MW01228287

For information, address:
FamiliesAlive®
PO Box 3288
Parker, CO 80134
www.familiesalive.org

First edition.

Scripture quotations are from The ESV® Bible (The Holy Bible, English
Standard Version®), copyright © 2001 by Crossway, a publishing
ministry of Good News Publishers. Used by permission. All rights
reserved.

ISBN: 978-1-946853-03-5
10 9 8 7 6 5 4 3 2 1

This book is dedicated to the parents, grandparents, and church leaders who are committed to raising the next generation to be followers of Christ.

I was a very young father when my wife, Ruth, and I discovered the treasures of God's grace. As we learned more about the Covenant of Grace that runs throughout the Scripture of the Old and New Testaments, we marveled at what was said about relationships in our lives. Our relationship with the Lord was transformed. Our understanding of human relationships changed as well.

But, most of all, our view of family relationships, especially of parenting, shifted dramatically. We moved from a place of bondage and fear to a place of trusting God for our children. This gave us great confidence that despite our own inadequacies and failures, God would be faithful to keep the promises of his relationship with us and with our children.

This workbook outlines some of the initial steps Ruth and I took in this journey of faith. It also outlines some of my teachings over the years to parents on their own journeys of faith.

I hope it will be an encouragement to you as you grow in faith, wrestle with your failings, and dedicate your family to God. I also hope it will equip you with practical tools to try in your own family.

Whether you use this as a self-study, for a Sunday School class, in a small group environment, or as a training guide for church staff, I pray that you, your children, and the children of your church will come to know, love, and serve the Lord in a deeper way.

Visit us at www.familiesalive.org for more encouragement and resources.

Rev. David Baer
President & CEO, FamiliesAlive®

Table of Contents

1

Living the Gospel

In a Nutshell...

Only when we ourselves are transformed by the Gospel can we be the types of parents that pass on the faith to our children.

What Do You Want?

At your core, what do you want for your children?

Do you want well-behaved kids? If so, this is not the book for you. There is a multitude of blogs, books, and research articles full of tips, tricks, and strategies for instilling good behavior.

But if you want children who are transformed by the love of the Father and the Good News of Jesus Christ, then you're in the right place.

We at FamiliesAlive want to dispel a myth for you: despite what you may have heard, there is no magic formula for raising kids of faith. But there is a great hope: Our God is a faithful God. He is the one who gifts faith and grace to those He calls. Moms, Dads, and grandparents who learn this about our Lord are those who live by the gospel of our Lord Jesus Christ. And it is these sorts of parents who are enabled to pass on the faith to the next generation.

Simply put, it doesn't depend on you. It depends on the God of grace, the only one who is faithful to save your children.

What is the Gospel?

When the Apostle Paul visited a city in the days of the early church, he had one goal: "I long to see you, that I may impart to you some spiritual gift to strengthen you" (Romans 1:11).

The spiritual gift Paul is referring to is the gospel of Jesus Christ. He preaches the gospel to the believers in Rome because "it is the power of God that brings salvation to everyone who believes: to the Jew first and also to the Greek. For in it the righteousness of God is revealed from faith for faith, as it is written, 'The righteous shall live by faith'" (Romans 1:16-17).

Contrary to what many people assume, the gospel is not just a free ticket to heaven that we earn when we say the Sinner's prayer. Rather, the gospel is the story of God at work throughout history, and it affects every aspect of our lives.

And living transformed lives as a result of this good news is where we must begin the journey of parenting.

Maybe you are starting this study as a parent who is very unsure how you are going to handle the job of raising your children. Maybe you have relied on simple formulas or strategies to conquer the task of discipling your kids.

But that is the wrong way to look at the job God has given you.

Your job as a parent is to live out the good news of the gospel, to share a remarkable journey with your children learning about the heart of the Father.

So now the question is, are you yourself transformed by this gospel?

Read This Now Ephesians 1:3 - 2:10

God's Story Unpacked

Ephesians 1-2 lays out a radical understanding of what the good news includes, revealing the process of how God brings His children to faith.

According to the passage, if you are a believer, it is because:

- God the Father loved, chose, and adopted you.
- Jesus redeemed you through His death and resurrection.
- The Holy Spirit enabled you to believe and guarantees your future with God.

Let's unpack this a bit.

First, God the Father has blessed you with every spiritual blessing in Christ. This includes loving us and choosing us to be adopted as His children, according to His pleasure and will. He did these things before the world was made - before we had any choice in the matter. He did all of this for us, that it might be to the praise of His glory.

Second is the work of Jesus on our behalf. Long before we were born, at the right time in history, Jesus came to the earth, lived a perfect life, and willingly went to the cross to purchase our redemption. Because of that we are forgiven and made right with God. Through His sacrifice, God chooses us, adopting us as His sons and daughters.

Finally, we come to the work of the Holy Spirit. At the right time in our lives, He comes to us and through the hearing of the good news of salvation, we believe. At that moment, the Holy Spirit marks us, guaranteeing our inheritance and future until we are forever with the Lord. Like everything else, this is God's work and not ours - and it is to the praise of His glory.

Taken together, this exposition from Ephesians reveals how God has worked throughout history to save us, His children.

Paul follows with a remarkable summary of the gospel message:

Because of His love for us, the God who is rich in mercy made us alive with Christ. Although we were dead, He made us alive with Jesus. By God's grace we have been saved. The life we have now is with Christ our Savior as surely as if we were seated with Him at God's right hand. God has done all this so that for eternity we might show the amazing riches of His grace, expressed in His kindness to us in Christ Jesus.

Take a moment to let this story, this good news, sink in. Let it excite you and stir your heart to praise the Lord for what He has done! No other response is possible.

Gospel-Centric Parenting

Why should we be concerned with raising children who understand the gospel, rather than well-behaved children? Hear this from Ephesians 2:

"For by grace you have been saved through faith. And this is not your own doing; it is the gift of God, not a result of works, so that no one may boast. For we are his workmanship, created in Christ Jesus for good works, which God prepared beforehand, that we should walk in them" (Ephesians 2:8-9).

This is why our goal is not simply to raise well-behaved children! We do not want children who blindly obey an arbitrary set of rules. Nor do we want our children to believe that by doing good works, they can earn salvation.

On the contrary, God did all the work necessary for our salvation. We can't take any credit, and He deserves all the praise.

The amazing truth of the Gospel is that we can't do it on our own. We are a mess! But the God of the universe is so full of love, mercy, and grace for us that He made a way. We need the gospel, not just to get into heaven, but as we live our lives moment by moment, day by day.

This story changes everything! It changes how we view ourselves, how we see the world, how we interact with others, and how we live out our lives. This is the story we want to tell our children. For if our children really understand this, they will be transformed.

Parents, you are not the solution for your children. Because you too are simply on the journey of faith. The best you can do is to be transformed yourself by this story. Then, you can introduce your children to our faithful, loving, and gracious God and walk alongside them as they embark on their own faith journey.

Ready, Set, Discuss

What is your story of coming to faith? How has your life been transformed by the Gospel? How can your life be further transformed by the Gospel?

_____

_____

_____

Now You Try!

- How does the Gospel message influence your parenting right now? Write out a brief answer to this question. It can be a few words, a few sentences, or a few paragraphs long. Hold on to your writing because we'll revisit it at the end of this study.
- Have your children tell you the story of Jesus. Can they articulate it at an age-appropriate level? Do they understand it at a heart-level? Whether they know and understand a lot or a little, practice sharing the Good News together.

Notes

2

Know, Love, & Serve

In a Nutshell...

We will never be perfect parents, but we can model to our children how to know, love, and serve the Lord.

A Simple Parenting Model

So, if there is no simple formula for raising kids of faith, and the secret is not found in our own perfection, where do we begin as parents?

When teaching children, I often remind kids that what God desires of them is pretty simple: "God wants you to know Him, and as you come to know Him, really know Him, you will fall in love with Him deeply. When you love Him, you will want to serve Him."

Know, love, and serve. That's what the Christian life is all about, and that is what we can model for our children.

Know, Love, and Serve: A Biblical Perspective

Put simply, the Know, Love and Serve model can be boiled down to this summary:

Know: As we spend time with God through reading His Word and in prayer, we come to know His character.

Love: As our knowledge of who God is grows, we fall in love with His grace, goodness, and love.

Serve: When we are captivated by love for the Father, serving God is a natural expression of our gratitude, a joyful response to our relationship with Him.

Let's break this down and look at what Scripture has to say.

Know

The apostle John wrote, "...this is eternal life, that they know you, the only true God, and Jesus Christ whom you have sent" (John 17:3). This is the starting place for the Christian life. Our God is so amazing that we can study Him and His Word for a lifetime without plumbing the depths of who He is. As the apostle Paul prayed for the Ephesians, "I do not cease to give thanks for you, remembering you in my prayers, that the God of our Lord Jesus Christ, the Father of glory, may give you the Spirit of wisdom and of revelation in the knowledge of him" (Ephesians 1:16-17).

Love

Later in Ephesians, Paul goes on to pray that this knowledge of God would also include an understanding of just how much God loves His children. "That you, being rooted and grounded in love, may have strength to comprehend with all the saints what is the breadth and length and height and depth, and to know the love of Christ that surpasses knowledge, that you may be filled with all the fullness of God" (Eph. 3:17b-19).

When a person really begins to understand the character of the God who loves us more than we can ever know, the most natural thing in the world is to fall in love with Him. "See what kind of love the Father has given to us, that we should be called children of God; and so we are… We love because he first loved us" (1 John 3:1a, 4:19). Loving God is a natural response to knowing God intimately.

Serve

Finally, this love shows itself in true service and obedience to the Lord. When we love God, serving Him is not an obligation bound in legalism, or an item to cross off our to-do list, but rather a joyful expression of our gratitude to Him. Worshipping God on Sundays is one way that we serve Him. We also serve Him when we practice a daily devotional life and teach our kids to do the same.

But serving God also means serving others. Our Savior came "not to be served, but to serve" (Mark 10:45). Becoming like Christ means mirroring that kind of service to others.

There are many ways to serve God by serving others as a family. You can teach them about tithing - giving money to God's work - and help them practice with their own allowances.

You can look for opportunities to serve at your church, or participate in a service project together - painting houses, volunteering at a food bank, cooking a meal for someone with a new baby, or filling a shoebox for Operation Christmas Child. Even small children can participate in these ways.

You can serve spontaneously - buying a meal for someone in need, or offering a hug, prayer, or kind word to someone hurting.

Remember, these service opportunities are not about doing what we are "supposed to" - but rather, joyfully responding to the Gospel message by showing God's love to others.

Parents who Know, Love, and Serve

Teaching our children the Know, Love, and Serve model is a wonderful way to give them an unshakeable foundation in faith.

What is wonderful about integrating this model in our families is that it is not about our own perfection - it's all about being in relationship with God. As we learned in the last chapter, none of us measure up as perfect parents. That's what the Gospel is all about. That's why Jesus came to the earth. He died and rose again to forgive our sins and reconcile us to the Father. Until we meet Him face-to-face, we will never be perfect.

Since it isn't about our perfection, we can help our children grow in a thriving relationship with the Lord by living transparent and authentic lives, seeking ourselves to know, love, and serve the Lord and giving them opportunities to do the same. As they see you, a humble, broken person, being transformed by the gospel, their hearts will blossom in the same kind of relationship with the Lord. As you seek to know, love, and serve the Lord, however imperfectly, your children will be drawn to this authenticity.

Know, Love, and Serve. That's what the Christian life is all about, and it's what will help our children develop a deep and meaningful relationship with God. Whether you grew up in a family who practiced this well or not at all, whether you have extensive Biblical training or are a brand-new Christian, this is a simple place to start.

Read This Now Psalm 100; Matthew 25:31-46

Ready, Set, Discuss

What do you already do at home to help your children know, love, and serve God?

How can you help your child know God better? What about loving and worshipping God? How about serving the Lord and others?

_____

_____

_____

Now You Try!

Over the next week or two, pick one activity that fits each category of the model to do together as a family. Make up your own or choose one of the sample activities from below.

Know

- Play Bible Quiz. Choose age-appropriate questions and give points for right answers.
- Give your kids a Bible passage and have them race to look it up in their Bibles.
- Play Pictionary or Charades with a twist: drawing and acting out Bible stories and characters.

Love

- Have a worship service at home. Let everyone pick one of their favorite songs to sing.
- Provide art supplies and have everyone create something themed around their favorite Bible verse.
- Go around the table and have everyone share things they are grateful for.
- List out all the attributes of God you can think about.

Serve

- Make and deliver a meal for a new mom or someone who recently had surgery.
- Help an elderly neighbor with some yard work.
- Volunteer at a soup kitchen together.

Notes

3

Your Most Important Job, Part 1

In a Nutshell...

Our job is to teach our children. The best way to teach is to MODEL and PRACTICE. We show them how it's done and we invite them to practice it.

Your Most Important Job

As a parent, what is your role in passing the faith to your children? Deuteronomy 6 sums it up in one word: *teach*.

"Hear, O Israel: The LORD our God, the LORD is one. You shall love the LORD your God with all your heart and with all your soul and with all your might. And these words that I command you today shall be on your heart. You shall *teach* them diligently to your children..." (Deut. 6:4-7a, emphasis added).

Teaching is the most important job for a parent. No other task is more critical. It requires commitment, intentionality, and diligence. This isn't optional. You can't opt out if you don't feel like it, if you're too tired, or if you aren't prepared enough. You can't drop your kids off at church for a few hours a week and leave all the teaching to a Sunday School teacher or youth pastor. The Bible makes it clear that teaching your children is your job. No one else can influence your children for Christ the way you can. It demands your priority.

Read This Now Deuteronomy 6:4-25

Five Adjectives

So, now we know *what* our most important job as parents is. Now the question remains: *How* do we teach our children about God? There are 5 adjectives I would like us to look at that summarize the kind of teaching God expects of parents: Intentional, Spontaneous, Creative, Redemptive, and Authentic. In this chapter, we will unpack the first three adjectives. We'll look at the last two adjectives in the chapter that follows.

Intentional

Moses told parents that they were to "diligently" teach their children (verse 7).

Intentional teaching means setting aside time each week for prayer, worship, Bible reading, and devotions. In our busy world and hectic schedules, this isn't easy - but our constant busyness is exactly why intentionality is so important.

Perhaps you can get together after dinner every Tuesday or Thursday. Or maybe the breakfast table works best in your schedule, or right before bedtime.

Whatever it is, figure out what works best for you and try to stick with it. But, at the same time don't stress out if things sometimes come up that change what you planned to do. Just don't allow those interruptions to dominate family life all the time – keeping you from focusing on what's important.

In my family, I found there were times when busyness started making any kind of family worship hard. When that happens to your devotional life together you may need to take extreme measures. For us, one of the ways we maintained our sanity and kept our closeness to each other and the Lord was by camping out. We would head to a state or national park – away from screens and technology. Worship and teaching times were always a meaningful part of these trips. Do what works best for your family to avoid the tyranny of the urgent.

Spontaneous

Just like you must intentionally set aside time to teach your children about God, much of your teaching can also be spontaneous. "You...shall talk of them when you sit in your house, and when you walk by the way, and when you lie down, and when you rise" (Deut. 6:7).

Too many parents think of teaching as something for which they should have special talent and training. These parents often give up before they start or drop off their kids at church for someone else to teach them. But the passage in Deuteronomy tells us that much of a parent's teaching is not done in formal, seminar settings. While formal times may be valuable, much of the teaching a parent does is informal - spontaneously occurring in the ordinary living of life together with your children. You must look for those teachable moments that occur often during the time you spend with your children.

You can do this on the road as you're heading to church or away from it. But soccer moms and dads can also do it on the way to and from practice, asking a thoughtful question like, "How did you see Jesus at work today?" Jesus did a lot of His discipling while He and His disciples were on the road. You can too. When you see something beautiful in nature, take the opportunity to point your children to the Creator. When your children are struggling with something, seize the chance to tell them about the God who loves them deeply and teach them to pray and trust Him. When something great happens, take the opportunity to praise God and thank Him for His provision!

By the way, a lot of these conversations you won't even need to start. Kids have a lot of curiosity and constantly ask questions about all sorts of things, even spiritual things. These questions are perfect opportunities for teachable moments.

Creative

Teaching doesn't have to be boring. Engage your kids creatively! Maybe this means decorating your home with Scripture passages or printing out Bible verse coloring pages. Maybe it means following the Christian calendar and creating fun family traditions around important holidays.

But most of all, I would encourage you, to be creative in the way you approach God's Word. It is atrocious to make the Bible boring. The reason Scripture is 70-80% narrative is that everybody loves a story – especially children. However, gaps in cultural and historical context can make the Bible difficult to understand. Fight against that trend! Make up different voices for different characters. Vary who reads. Act out a passage together and even record them. Sing Bible verses. Turn Scripture memory into a game. It doesn't take a lot of time to try out different ways to approach God's word. A worship time should never feel like a rut you've fallen into.

Of course, the Bible is God's Word and we want to approach it with respect. But, even so, we can maintain a sense of humor and an atmosphere of fun!

An Example: Creativity in Church

Let me illustrate this with an example from my own life. Growing up, our daughters sat with us in church services every Sunday. To help them creatively engage their minds, we gave them scratch paper and encouraged them to write or draw what they heard.

Our oldest daughter was a wordsmith. As she listened to the sermon her job was to write down words the Pastor used that she didn't understand. Then, that afternoon we'd look over her list and help her to understand what the words and phrases meant.

By contrast, our second daughter has always been visually oriented. So, this daughter would draw pictures during the sermon. Later, we would talk about how they fit in with the pastor's message.

One Sunday, she drew herself with her arms outstretched and jelly beans in an arch over her in the sky. I looked at the picture, scratched my head, and couldn't figure out what that had to do with anything in the service that morning.

But she reminded me, "Daddy, those are the en-jelly beans that are all around us." We all got a good laugh, realizing she had misheard the pastor when he said "angelic beings" - Yes, the pastor had preached about the angels of God who are all around us watching over His children!

Don't be afraid to let your children engage creatively with God's Word, rooted in their unique, God-given gifts, talents, and interests. This freedom helps them develop a deeper love of God.

Ready, Set, Discuss

Do you see teaching your children as your most important task? How have you done so far as a parent?

_____

_____

_____

Which of these adjectives - intentional, spontaneous, and creative - comes most naturally when teaching your children? Which is the most challenging for you?

_____

_____

_____

Now You Try!

Each day over the next week, jot down a few teaching moments you had with your children in a notebook. Which of the 3 adjectives best describes that teaching moment? Record the applicable adjectives. Next week, we'll take a deeper look at the teaching journal.

Notes

4

Your Most Important Job, Part 2

In a Nutshell…

As parents, our most important job is to teach our children. In addition to being intentional, spontaneous, and creative, the best teaching is also redemptive and authentic.

Read this Now Psalm 78:1-18

Telling our Children

Psalm 78 is a great reminder that a parent's most important job is to teach their children about the Lord.

The psalmist is talking about the amazing things God has done for us when he says, "We will not hide them from their children, but tell to the coming generation the glorious deeds of the Lord, and his might, and the wonders that he has done." Why is it essential to do this? vs. 7-8 explain: "…so that they should set their hope in God and not forget the works of God, but keep His commandments; and that they should not be like their fathers, a stubborn and rebellious generation, a generation whose heart was not steadfast, whose spirit was not faithful to God."

The psalmist goes on to detail all the failures that took place when parents hid from the coming generation "the glorious deeds of the LORD, and his might, and the wonders that he has done." When the faithlessness of a generation is passed to the next generation the tendency is to stray further and further from the Lord. No wonder God would require those who demonstrated such a lack of faith to fall in the wilderness. Since the Lord had proved Himself mighty to save and had rescued His people from Egypt – He expected His people to respond in faith. Refusal to trust Him is not an option with which God will be pleased.

Yes, this requires a parent to be ready at any time and in any circumstance to respond to a child's questions. It also means sharing the good times and the hard times a family goes through in a transparent way so that your kids see first-hand how you live out your relationship with the Lord. In these circumstances, the most important thing is for you to be open and honest with how you are feeling. As they see how you handle things by God's grace and help, they will grow in their own character development.

In the last chapter, we looked at the Biblical charge for parents to teach their children about the Lord. We unpacked three characteristics of our teaching - *intentional, spontaneous,* and *creative.* Now, let's look at the last two characteristics, *redemptive* and *authentic.*

Redemptive

Teaching redemptively is an important concept that even many of our pastors, Sunday School teachers, and youth leaders miss the mark on.

Redemptive teaching means that everything is centered around the person and work of Jesus Christ. When we teach the Bible redemptively, we look at it as a whole, always connecting the passage back to how it fits into God's story of redemption. The opposite of redemptive teaching is moralistic teaching. Moralistic teaching looks at an individual Scripture and distills it down to a simple moral lesson - do this or don't do this.

Still a bit fuzzy? Let's look at the Ten Commandments as an example.

From a moralistic perspective, the Ten Commandments are simply a checklist of things that we should or should not do. However, from a redemptive perspective, the Ten Commandments are so much more! Understood in the context of God's story, we see that the Ten Commandments were given by God to His people, Israel. We also see the significance that no one could keep God's commands perfectly, which is why He sent His Son, Jesus, to die for us and purchase our redemption. We also understand that these commandments are God's loving rules that help His people to flourish. To this day, we live by these commandments - not out of obligation, but out of gratitude and a desire to serve Him.

Isn't that a huge difference? When we teach the Bible moralistically, we do a great disservice to our children - making it seem that the Bible is all about doing the right things. But, as we've already established, the Truth of the Scriptures is that all of us fail to honor the Lord! When we see our sin as God sees it, we know our only hope is in the Savior who died on the cross and who was raised from the dead for those who know and love Him. The Gospel is all about how God loved us and saved us despite our sin. That is the hope we hold out to our children.

Here's another example: When teaching our children, we could look at King David and his heart for God and say "Be like David!". Or we could look at the story of David's sin with Bathsheba and say "Don't be like David!". But these are moralistic, not redemptive teachings. A far more powerful teaching is to show how God worked in the life of David. Even when David failed God, God was with David and forgave him. One day, our Savior, Jesus, came from David's line and once and for all forgave us of our sin. Isn't this a much better message for our children to hear?

Authentic

The final characteristic is the most important one - we need to teach authentically. The word *authentic* really talks about your own walk with the Lord. We can teach our children all we want, but unless we are living out a vibrant faith, it won't mean much to our kids. Faith is more often caught than taught. *Not only do our children need to be taught the right stuff but they must see that right stuff in action.*

So how do we cultivate a vibrant, authentic faith that our children will see? The answer is wrapped up in our love for the Lord. Think about the first time you fell in love. Wasn't the person you loved always on your mind? This is what our God desires from His people. It is the first thing our Lord expects of believers who have been gifted with children.

In the Gospel of Mark, when Jesus is questioned by a scribe, "'Which commandment is the most important of all?'" Jesus answered, 'The most important is, 'Hear, O Israel: The Lord our God, the Lord is one. And you shall love the Lord your God with all your heart and with all your soul and with all your mind and with all your strength.'" He then adds, "The second is this: 'You shall love your neighbor as yourself.' There is no other commandment greater than these" (Mark 12:28-31).

What Jesus did in this statement was summarize and expand the teaching of Moses through the Ten Commandments. While they may seem like a boring set of rules, really, Jesus shows us that it is all about love for God and others. The first four commandments concern our relationship with God, and the last six have to do with our relationships with others. In the Old Testament, the people were to listen to them and fall deeply in love with the God who had given them. Only a passionate love would do. No wonder that Moses says, "these words that I command you today shall be on your heart" (verse 6).

When we are captivated by love for the Father, we will live out our faith authentically before the Lord and our children. This is great news, especially for new Christians! It isn't about perfection - it's about being genuine about your successes and failures. When your children see an authentic faith in their parents, struggles, victories, and all, they are drawn to it. In this way, you are on a spiritual journey with your children – and it is good for them to see you dealing with all the twists and turns along the way.

So being perfect is not what this passage is talking about. Rather, God desires truth in our inner thought life. He doesn't want anything that is counterfeit, fake or unreal. How can we really impact the lives of our children and help them to bring every thought captive to Christ (2 Corinthians 10:5) if we are not working to do the same?

So, make sure that you're honest and transparent before your children. It is one of the most important attributes for a child to discern regarding his parents. Children growing up in a home where the parent or parents are genuine in their own journey of faith and demonstrate integrity in their walk with the Lord are far more likely to continue the journey of faith on their own.

Ready, Set, Discuss

On the spectrum of moralistic to redemptive, where does your teaching tend to fall? How could you become more redemptive in the lessons you teach your children?

What is an important lesson God has taught you through your life experiences? How can you be more transparent with your children about your failings?

Now You Try!

Set aside some time to reflect on the teaching moments you recorded last week. Which teaching adjectives appear more often? Which teaching adjectives are lacking? Is your teaching more moralistic or redemptive? Is it more hypocritical or authentic? Spend some time in prayer that God will grow you as a parent as you tackle the task of teaching your children.

Notes

5

A Place of Grace

In a Nutshell...

God's relationship with us is one of unconditional love. Extending this type of relationship to our spouse and kids has the power to revolutionize family life.

Coping with Stress

Let's face it: Marriage and parenting are stressful.

Although marriage is a great thing, it is constantly listed as one of the most stressful life events because of the significance of that transition. Can you guess what another stressful life event is? Having a baby!

Studies show that the "honeymoon phase" of a marriage usually lasts about a year[1]. During that first year, for many, the relationship is blissful and rosy. But then, the glow wears off - all of a sudden, your spouse's quirks which once seemed adorable may become annoying, or differences in upbringing and disparate conflict styles cause

---

[1] Emanuele, Enzo & Politi, Pierluigi & Bianchi, Marika & Minoretti, Piercarlo & Bertona, Marco & Geroldi, Diego. (2006). Raised plasma nerve growth factor levels associated with early-stage romantic love. Psychoneuroendocrinology. 31. 288-94.

relational problems. For those that make it through those hurdles, becoming parents adds a whole new set of difficulties - you have another mouth to feed - one that cries often and keeps you up in the night, and requires all your attention.

How do you cope with the stress brought by getting married or the birth of a child? Maybe you grew up in a vibrant Christian family where good relationships were modeled for you. Many people (including me) did not have that advantage. Marriage teaches you quickly that you need to learn how to relate peacefully and cordially. But how?

The answer is a term that may or may not be familiar to you - *Covenant*. The Covenant of Grace is the thread that runs throughout all of the Old and New Testaments and is the heart of the story of God and His people.

To understand the centrality of the covenant of grace in our relationship with God and others, let's first define what a covenant is and isn't.

Covenant vs. Contract

Contract - A contract is a conditional agreement between two parties. If one party does not hold up their end of a contract, the contract is no longer legally binding, and the other party is not obligated to hold up their end.

Covenant - In contrast, *covenant* is an unconditional promise made in the context of a meaningful relationship. If you have entered into a covenant, you are bound to that promise unconditionally, regardless of how the other party acts.

As we will see in a moment, God's relationship with us is one of *covenant*. And He asks us to model this same unconditional love and promises within our families, transforming our homes into places of grace.

Read This Now Genesis 15

The Covenant of Grace

We first see the Covenant of Grace at work in Genesis 15, when God came to Abraham, who was still known as Abram at the time. The Lord spoke to him, "Fear not, Abram, I am your shield; your reward shall be very great." But Abram said, "O Lord GOD, what will you give me, for I continue childless...?" (Gen. 15:1-2). Abraham was concerned because God had promised him an heir. In fact, God had promised him many children! But, even though Abraham and his wife were growing old, they still had no children.

So, the Lord took Abraham outside and said, "'Look toward heaven, and number the stars, if you are able to number them.'" Then He said to him, 'So shall your offspring be.' And he believed the LORD, and He counted it to him as righteousness" (Gen. 15:5-6)

Did you catch that? There was nothing else for Abraham to do. He simply believed. That was all he did.

Later in the chapter, God wanted to show Abraham that He would do what He had promised. So He asked Abraham to cut a heifer, goat, and ram in half and set the halves opposite each other.

While this seems weird to us today, Abraham would have understood exactly what was happening. In those Old Testament days, when two powerful tribal leaders came to an agreement and wanted to bind themselves to keep that agreement, the two would walk between the halved carcasses together, saying something like, "If I fail to keep my word to you, may this be what happens to me!" It was a powerful symbol, showing that the two of them would keep their promises - and the penalty for not upholding this contract was death.

Abraham would have known this context. He and God were making an unbreakable contract with each other.

Then, God did something unexpected. God put Abraham into a deep, trance-like sleep. Then, after speaking in detail about His promise, in the form of a smoking oven and flaming torch, God passed between the halved carcasses all by Himself.

The fact that God walked between the pieces signified that the total commitment for fulfilling the agreement was God's alone - a unique covenant relationship. No matter what Abraham did or failed to do, God would uphold His promises.

The significance of this story for us is that God's promise to Abraham is one that extends to us today. He offers His people this sort of covenant relationship. That is why it is called the covenant of *grace* - because it doesn't depend on what we do. No matter how many times we fail, God still loves us and stays in relationship with us. None of us can strike a bargain with God or make a contract with Him or cut a covenant with the Lord as though we are His equal. We are dependent on His grace to fulfill the terms of the covenant.

We get to be in right relationship with God - and it has nothing to do with us. It is all because He fulfills the terms of the covenant all by Himself. Also significant: the dead animals point forward in time when another sacrifice would be made, one that assures the promises of God to His people are unconditional and last for all time. The sacrifice we refer to is the Lord Jesus, crucified on the cross for us.

Now the implication of this covenant of grace says so much about our relationship to God. We can't do anything to receive His promises, but simply to accept His grace and believe. We rest, we trust, we sleep in His grace.

Because of His grace, we have come to know unconditional love. We are accepted just as we are, far less than perfect. God will never give up on us and leave us behind. We also know unconditional love and mercy. This love does not treat us as our sins deserve, but because of Christ, we are forgiven. After all, the punishment we deserved, was laid upon Him. Our debts are canceled.

It is God making a promise or commitment to His people that is unconditional. This covenant is usually expressed in the Bible in these formulaic words: "I will be your God and you will be my people."

All along, God knew that His people would fail and sin and break any vows they might make to Him. But He is the God who is faithful to His word.

It is so critical that we understand the covenant concept in the Bible, lest we falsely believe that our relationship with God is one of a contract, dependent on us. Truth be told, we have nothing with which to bargain. It is God and God alone who pledges Himself to us in the Covenant of Grace.

The Covenant Home

So what does this mean for our family life? How do we make our homes places of this kind of grace? How can we embrace something different? Could we have a distinctly covenant kind of family? A covenant of grace kind of family?

That is exactly what the Bible teaches a family should look like. The amazing application of all of this is that all our family relationships now become something more. Marriage means more than just a civil ceremony or contract that any party can leave at will. We cannot say, "You don't make me happy anymore, our marriage is over!"

Jesus rightly came along and condemned this practice by the Pharisees, calling divorce not pleasing to the Lord (cf. Matthew 19:1-10). This is because marriage is to be viewed as a covenant - a life-long commitment to love and stay in relationship together, whether the other person deserves it or not (cf. Malachi 2:10-16)[2]. The Malachi passage also teaches the importance of only marrying someone who also loves the Lord. And the reason why you should

---

[2] **Note:** While we believe marriage is a life-long, covenantal commitment, we also recognize that some find themselves in abusive situations or facing spousal unfaithfulness. These things are wrong, and if you find yourself here, please seek out your pastor or a trained Christian counselor who can provide guidance in your situation.

only marry a fellow believer is that the Lord desires godly offspring to be raised in these covenant families.

Just as our wedding vows are part of our marriage covenant with our spouse, our relationship with our children is viewed as a covenant relationship as well. When we bring our children to be baptized, we make vows before the Lord. Within the context of a covenant relationship, we bring our children, by our vows, not theirs, into a relationship with the Lord and with the local church to which we belong. By the way, the church also enters into covenant with us and our children as the entire congregation makes a vow to our children.

When we view all of family life not as a conditional contract, but as a covenant relationship, something wonderful is unleashed in the relationship of a husband and wife, and in the relationship of a father and mother and their children. Just as God deals by grace with us we are now empowered to deal by grace with our loved ones. As parents, this means we begin to develop an *unconditional love* that is OK with accepting less than perfection in ourselves and our children. It also stops taking everything as an affront to ourselves personally and never gives up or quits on a child.

Also, this view of the covenant unleashes an *unconditional acceptance* that accepts differences and says we can still be one together. This kind of unity and inclusiveness and diversity never pushes away or rejects someone from relationship with us.

Additionally, when we look at our family relationships as covenantal, we see that we are called to *unconditional mercy and forgiveness*. We don't respond with judgment, but with mercy to our family members. We forgive rather than punish.

Let's be clear - this does not mean we do not discipline our children. Children learn how to live in right relationship with God and others by experiencing consequences for their actions. However, Godly discipline is neither abusive nor overly harsh. We learn in Hebrews that "the Lord disciplines the one he loves, and chastises every son whom he receives" (Heb. 12:6). God's discipline towards us doesn't change his love for us. In fact, it is an act of love. Likewise, we discipline our children because we want what's best for them. But our love, forgiveness, mercy, and acceptance for our spouse or children should never be based on their performance.

God has extended a covenant of grace to us. Let's extend that to our families as we make our homes a place of grace.

Ready, Set, Discuss

How was parenting and family life modeled for you growing up? Were unconditional love and covenant relationships present in your upbringing?

_____

_____

_____

How might your parenting look different if you viewed your spouse and your children through the lens of a covenant relationship?

_____

_____

_____

Now You Try!

Gather up and write a family covenant together. Explain to your children at an age-appropriate level the concept of covenant - that you are committing to love one another unconditionally, just like God has done for you. The family covenant will sound a lot like wedding vows - promises you are all making to each other. Let each person contribute to the discussion, with mom and dad making the final decision about what to include. When finished, type up your covenant, print it out, have everyone sign it, and frame it in a prominent place in your home.

Notes

6

God-like Love

In a Nutshell...

The love and forgiveness of God are what enables us to love and forgive our children.

Read This Now Psalm 103

Hesed

I have always treasured the Hebrew word *hesed*. It is full of meaning. In English Bibles it is translated in different ways: sometimes as love, mercy, kindness, compassion, faithfulness, loyalty and even grace. To convey the rich meaning of hesed, the King James Bible translators even invented a new word: lovingkindness.

We don't have a word in English to capture everything that hesed is. However, the key idea is that God's love for us is never-ending, unconditional, and all-encompassing.

I learned an important message about God's hesed when I spent a month in Uganda on a short-term mission trip. In my first message to those gathered in Uganda, I was preaching from Psalm 103, trying to express the richness of God's love by sharing the various meanings of the word hesed, and I was a novice in preaching with an interpreter. As I used all the English words that were expressed in hesed (mercy, forgiveness, compassion, faithfulness, etc.) I suddenly realized that my translator was just using the same word again and again. I must have sounded like a broken record.

Afterward, I asked my translator why he just kept saying the same thing. He replied by telling me that the regional language was a small dialect with very few words compared to English. Only one Ugandan word meant all those things I had said. I thought, "Duh, just like the Hebrew used by David!"

The concept that God's love is rich and unending for those who belong to Him is remarkable, no matter the language used to express it! It explains why God would go to such great lengths to reverse the effects of the fall and redeem us to Himself.

The Apostle Paul describes how this kind of love expresses itself in 1 Corinthians 13:

"Love is patient and kind; love does not envy or boast; it is not arrogant or rude. It does not insist on its own way; it is not irritable or resentful; it does not rejoice at wrongdoing, but rejoices with the truth. Love bears all things, believes all things, hopes all things, endures all things. Love never ends" (1 Cor. 13:4–8).

God has always demonstrated this kind of remarkable love for His children. As a parent, this is significant for two reasons: First, it helps you understand your relationship with God and second, it shows you how you should view the precious child or children the Lord has granted you.

Love As Christ Loved Us

In the gospels, we frequently see Christ ministering to children. In Matthew 19, parents brought their children to Him that He might lay His hands on them and pray. The disciples thought this was a distraction and rebuked the parents. But Jesus had a different plan.

"Let the little children come to me and do not hinder them, for to such belongs the kingdom of heaven," He said (Matt. 19:14).

In Mark 9, it is reported that Jesus "took a child and put him in the midst of them, and taking him in his arms, he said to them, 'Whoever receives one such child in my name receives me, and whoever receives me, receives not me but him who sent me'" (Mark 9:36-37).

Christian parents who are wise will try to mirror the Lord's kind of love to their children. This is not easy to do. In fact, it is impossible to do this perfectly! But as you seek God, you will grow as a parent. As you receive His love, you will be better able to love your own children. As you encounter His forgiveness, you will learn to forgive and seek forgiveness for your own failures. You can change from being envious, irritable, arrogant, rude, boastful and any of the other many ways sin shows itself in your life.

Case Study: Anger

Practically speaking, how can God's *hesed* love transform our sinful responses into a deep and abiding love for our children? One issue that damages many marriages and parent-child relationships is anger - so let's use that as an illustration.

In the book of Ephesians, the Apostle Paul teaches us how to keep anger from boiling over in your relationships. "Be kind to one another, tenderhearted, forgiving one another, as God in Christ forgave you. Therefore be imitators of God, as beloved children. And walk in love, as Christ loved us and gave himself up for us, a fragrant offering and sacrifice to God" (Eph. 4:32–5:2).

What Paul is saying here is that the secret to conquering anger is not to grit your teeth and just not be angry. Rather, we control our anger because of the amazing truth that God is not angry with us. In fact, Paul says that God loves us deeply and He forgives us "in Christ." God doesn't look at our hearts to find a reason to forgive us. What a relief! Instead, He looks to the work of Jesus Christ on the cross nearly two thousand years ago. Because of Christ's sacrifice, we get to encounter God's full forgiveness instead of His anger.

So when you find it hard to be like the Lord in His unending lovingkindness - *hesed* - because either your spouse or child has done something that really bothers you, stop looking at them to find a reason to forgive them. Instead, look at what Jesus has done for you and others – and on that basis, forgive the one who has wronged you or disobeyed. For no other reason than the work of Christ. That is forgiving others as God has forgiven you. It is an expression of unconditional and unending love made possible by Christ, and it is the quickest way to dispel anger.

Ready, Set, Discuss

Name a time that you experienced remarkable love and forgiveness. How did that impact you?

How can you better extend the love and forgiveness of Christ to your children?

Now You Try!

Sometime this week, gather together as a family. Provide some small slips of paper and let each person write a sin they have committed or they struggle with. This could be specific (I called my sister a mean name) or general (disrespect). Light a candle, and have everyone crumple up their slip of paper and burn it. Discuss God's love and forgiveness - that He takes away our sins, making them disappear like the slips of paper you burned in the candle.

Notes

7

Coaching Champions

In a Nutshell...

if we want children who know, love, and serve the Lord throughout their lives, we must start coaching early.

An Example from Golf

Tiger Woods is among the most successful and well-known golfers of all time. Before he was a year old, his dad, Earl Woods, cut down a putter for his size and had Tiger start walking around with it. A few months later he started swinging a driver. And the rest is history. Earl, Tiger's dad, is credited with Tiger's early development as a champion golfer.

In fact, there are many parents throughout history who can be credited, at least in part, for their child's successes. Tennis stars Venus and Serena Williams' father, Richard, wrote up a 78-page plan and began coaching his daughters by the age of four. Even Ludwig van Beethoven developed into a piano prodigy at the constant training from his father, Johann, and theoretical physicist Stephen

Hawking's parents both put a high value on education and pushed him to succeed academically.

While you may disagree with these parents' methods, they teach us an important lesson: Coaching a champion starts early – and parents are of vital importance to their development. If we want children who will grow up to be pro athletes (or musicians, or theoretical physicists), we must start them young.

If this is true of sports, arts, and academics, it is even truer when it comes to the spiritual life of our children. Recent research from the Barna group suggests that almost 80% of American Christians accepted Christ before the age of 21. They also found that those who accepted Christ before the teen years are most likely to remain absolutely committed to the faith, and that faith habits form early and change surprisingly little over time. Many studies have shown that evangelism and discipleship are most effective when undertaken by parents of children between the ages of 4-14.

Simply put, if we want children who know, love, and serve the Lord throughout their lives, we must start coaching early.

Read This First Ephesians 6:1-4

Biblical Family Life

Have you turned on the TV lately? From series like *The Simpsons* and *Mad Men* to commercials and ads, Dad figures everywhere are portrayed as somewhere on the spectrum from idiot to absent, with mouthy children who are usually better off if they ignore his advice, which they regularly do.

In Ephesians 6, the Apostle Paul paints a picture of family life that is in sharp contrast to the picture of the American family. First, Paul addresses the kind of attitude children should have toward their parents. They are called to obey, honor, and respect parents and others who are in positions of authority over them.

Then, the Apostle Paul turns his attention to the fathers, calling them to a role far beyond that of society's bumbling, absent dad. Note that what Paul says is applicable to dads and moms, and anyone with a primary caregiver role for a child. But dads should take a lead in making sure this happens in his family![3]

Each aspect of Paul's advice to parents is vital in helping us coach our children in their spiritual development. Let's take a look at five key phrases from Ephesians 6 that will help us grow as spiritual coaches.

Bring Them Up

First, consider the phrase *bring them up*. This is more than just having and raising children. It is about nourishing the spiritual life of your children and helping them to flourish in it.

In our work with families, we have noticed two common myths about child-rearing that we would like to dispel.

The first myth is that it is best to remain neutral and let children decide for themselves what they think about Christianity.

Unfortunately, the results of this parenting choice are like having a garden that you never weed. After a while, it's not going to look like a garden at all. The weeds will have choked out anything the garden would have produced. As children grow up, their spiritual life needs to be tended to just like we would tend to a garden.

The second myth is that it's better to leave the spiritual coaching of your children to the professionals. Many Christian parents rely entirely on their church's kids program or youth group to teach them about God. They're the experts, after all!

Imagine if you only gave your child a meal one or two times a week - they would quickly waste away to nothing. The same thing happens

---

[3]We live in a broken world where families everywhere are impacted by divorce, abuse, and neglect. Not every child grows up in a two-parent home. Often, the task of bringing up children in the Lord falls to a single parent, a grandparent, a step-parent, a foster parent or one believing parent. Whatever the case may be, God knows your situation and His grace will fill in the gaps. Being involved in a local church is a great way to surround your family with role models to help impact your family life.

spiritually when our children are only fed once or twice a week at church. Make no mistake: the local church plays a crucial role in helping your child grow in faith. But it was never meant to be the primary or only method.

If you want your child to be a world-class athlete, they need to be brought up in the sport. One or two times a week would never cut it. If you want your child to be a spiritual champion, the same rules apply.

Training

Specifically, Paul calls dads to bring up children in *training*. The Greek word used here indicates the sort of training of children used in the Paideia school movement - with a focus on drills, repetition, and memory work. The connection to coaching is obvious. For children to grow as athletes, they must run drills, practice again and again, and develop muscle memory. The same must happen in their spiritual lives if we want our children to develop, and parents play an important role in their child's spiritual training.

Instruction

According to Paul, we also bring up our children in *instruction*, a word that literally means "warnings".

Practically speaking, this is all about showing your children the wisdom of God's Word. It is about teaching them the natural consequences of sinful choices. It is about sharing honestly from your experience - your successes and failures - in following God. It is about saying to them, "here is what happens when..."

These teaching moments along the way are valuable. Don't think that instruction is boring! Think of yourself as your child's coach, for that is what God is calling you to be.

When you coach your child to ride a bike, you instruct them not to pedal too slow. When you coach them to swing a baseball bat, you warn them against swinging up instead of swinging level. When you coach them to throw a football, you remind them to keep their fingers on the laces. When you coach them to walk with the Lord, you warn them about the pitfalls they might face.

Do Not Provoke Your Children to Anger

Paul also reminds fathers not to provoke their children to anger. There is nothing more demoralizing than a coach who tears us down. A great coach knows how to encourage, offer constructive criticism, and bring out the best in their players. Seek to be that kind of coach! The best way to evaluate yourself is to ask: What am I doing to make my kids angry? In what ways do I turn my child away from the Lord and His grace?

When it comes to parenting, we have found five main areas in which parents tend to either turn their children towards anger or turn them towards the Lord. Each of these areas is a sliding scale. We all land in slightly different places, and we will never be perfect, but the goal is to move away from the behaviors on the left and towards those on the right as we develop into great spiritual coaches.

Check out the spectrums below - where do you fit on each one?

Hypocritical  Authentic

Hypocritical parents hold their children to one moral standard, while not upholding it themselves. This double standard is confusing and breeds resentment. Authentic parents practice what they preach and are vulnerable about their struggles. Hypocrisy breeds resentment in children, while an authentically-lived faith is attractive to them.

Harsh  Gentle

Harsh parents use cruel punishments, verbal tirades, and sometimes physical abuse to obtain absolute obedience, which generates anger especially in the teen years. Gentle parents are able to enforce rules and discipline their children while showing love and maintaining trust.

Absent  Present

Parents who are absent, physically or emotionally, deprive children of much-needed nurture and, as a result, their instruction is often dismissed and resented. Present parents model the love of God our Father and their instruction will be better received.

Discouraging  Encouraging

Discouraging parents are negative and critical toward their kids, causing children to seek acceptance and value elsewhere. Encouraging parents ensure a child knows their worth and who their worth comes from.

Indulgent  Authoritative

Indulgent parents fail to discipline their children or provide guidelines and rules for them. Authoritative parents set clear boundaries and hold their children accountable to these standards. Ultimately, children who grow up in authoritative (not authoritarian) households are more likely to be responsible, well-adjusted, and on a good trajectory for their life.

In & Of The Lord

Finally, all of this coaching takes place *in the Lord* (verse 1) and is *of the Lord* (verse 4). When we talk about faith being passed down through the generations, never forget that it is God who makes this all work. He blesses the institution of the family. He makes up for all our failures and shortcomings. He keeps His promises. That is His very nature! When coaching your children feels overwhelming, remember that it is all about His faithfulness.

Ready, Set, Discuss

Of the five sliding scales, on which do you operate most towards the left side (provoking children to anger)? On which do you operate most towards the right side (turning children to the Lord)?

How does the metaphor of coaching inform your role in your children's spiritual life?

Now You Try!

Imagine your family is a sports team, and you are the head coach. Create a coaching plan for your team. What are your current team's strengths and weaknesses? What are your goals? What short-term and long-term strategies might you employ to achieve those goals? What drills and activities might you run to develop your team?

Notes

8

The Priesthood of Parents

In a Nutshell…

In Christ, we have been chosen into a royal priesthood. As parents, we are called to be family priests, guiding and leading our children spiritually.

Read This Now 1 Peter 2:4-10

If you wrote the job description for being a parent, would "priestly duties" make the list? I bet not before today!

What Peter says in the passage we just read makes it clear that followers of Jesus have been chosen into a new priesthood, which makes us priests.

What does this mean exactly? We believe that Moms and Dads are called by God to be priests to their children. In Bible times, priests led God's people in worship, prayed with and for God's people, and pronounced blessings over them, as well. In the same way, parents are called to perform these priestly roles in their family. We'll look at each of these in turn.

Family Worship

The first priestly role of the parent is in leading family worship. As Peter makes clear, the reason God has chosen us as a royal priesthood is to "proclaim the excellencies of him who called you out of darkness into his marvelous light" (1 Pet. 2:9). This surely speaks of worship.

Worshipping God is not just something we do at church. As your family's priest, make your home a place where the greatness of God is talked about. Marvel at the beauty of sunrises and sunsets. Praise Him for the beauty you see in nature. Sing worship songs and hymns together. Even a trip to the zoo is an opportunity to wonder at and worship the Creator. Let me share a story: when our girls were age two and three, we took a trip to the Brookfield Zoo in Chicago and it was extraordinary. I still remember the exclamations coming from the strollers: "Look what else God made! He's amazing!"

Leading your family in worship also means reading the Bible together. You may feel unequipped to approach a narrative you find in the Bible. Just remember that from beginning to end the Bible is God's Story. Look for how He is acting in the story and proclaim His excellencies!

Praying With and For Your Children

Another crucial role you take on as a family priest is praying with and for your children. You can start praying for them even before they are born, and as they are formed in the womb. Pray that God gives them His Spirit to make them alive spiritually from an early age.

I often think of David's words in Psalm 22: "Yet you are he who took me from the womb; you made me trust you at my mother's breasts. On you was I cast from my birth, and from my mother's womb you have been my God" (Psalm 22:9-10). How wonderful would it be if, like David, your children cannot remember a time when they didn't know or love the Lord?

What else should you pray for? Pray that the blessings found in the covenant of grace are made real in their lives. Psalm 103:17-18 talks about these blessings: "But the steadfast love of the LORD is from everlasting to everlasting on those who fear him, and his righteousness to children's children, to those who keep his covenant and remember to do his commandments".

You can also pray over them Paul's prayer from Ephesians 1, "that the God of our Lord Jesus Christ, the Father of glory, may give you the Spirit of wisdom and of revelation in the knowledge of him, having the eyes of your hearts enlightened, that you may know what is the hope to which he has called you, what are the riches of his glorious inheritance in the saints, and what is the immeasurable greatness of his power toward us who believe, according to the working of his great might that he worked in Christ when he raised him from the dead and seated him at his right hand in the heavenly places, far above all rule and authority and power and dominion, and above every name that is named, not only in this age but also in the one to come. And he put all things under his feet and gave him as head over all things to the church, which is his body, the fullness of him who fills all in all" (Eph. 1:17–23).

Pray for every aspect of their lives. Pray for their success in school, pray for good friends, for safety as they play or travel. Pray for every thought they might have, that they might bring it into submission to Christ. Pray for their future wife or husband, pray often for the spouses the Lord is preparing for them. Pray that they, too, will stay pure and love the Lord with all their heart, soul and mind.

Why, you can even pray for future generations yet to come, that your children's children and generations more will love and serve the Lord. In your earnest prayers lifted to God, you will be a faithful priest for your kids.

But, don't only pray *for* your children. Pray *with* them as well, teaching them to pray. In Matthew 6, Jesus teaches His disciples how to pray. You can use the Lord's Prayer to teach your children to pray at a very early age. Teach them to praise him, to hallow (honor) His name. Teach them to pray for His will to be done. Teach them to ask and thank God for His provision of food. Help them to ask for forgiveness and for help in forgiving others. Pray together for freedom from evil. Using Jesus' example is the best way to teach them how to pray.

Finally, you should also pray for yourself, asking God to help you become a better parent. Ask God to deepen your love for your children. Ask Him to help you become more patient and kind and holy in all your ways. Perfection is not required, but as your children see God's transforming work in your heart and life they will begin to understand their own calling to be priests as well.

Blessing your Children

As family priests, parents also have the opportunity to bless their children. The practice of blessing is not that common nowadays, but we think it is worth consideration.

God Himself originated the idea of blessing. He told Abraham that he and his children were called to be a blessing to the nations. In Christ, this is fulfilled in all believers and their children. This calling to bless others is one that is passed down from generation to generation.

In the book of Deuteronomy, when Aaron was called to be the high priest, he and his sons were instructed to bless God's children. What's more, we see examples of priests pronouncing blessings over God's people throughout Scripture. And as we belong to the royal priesthood through Christ, we get to be a part of passing this blessing onto our children.

Blessing your children is as simple as placing your hand on their head and pronouncing Scripture over them. But it has an impact that is almost impossible to overestimate.

Children who are regularly blessed by their parents report feeling a certain sense of safety, security, and protection in their lives. A little girl once told me that when her parents blessed her, it was "sort of like a hug to my head." The practice is so meaningful to kids that when they are older, they almost universally report that they plan to do the same thing with their children.

Ready, Set, Discuss

Do you see yourself as the family priest, responsible for the spiritual leadership of your family?

How do you already practice family worship, praying for and with your children, or blessing your children in your home? What, if anything, would be beneficial to add?

Now You Try!

Take time to read the following blessings present throughout Scripture. Choose a favorite or two. As you tuck your children in tonight, place your hand upon their heads and pronounce the blessing out loud.

Biblical Blessings

- "The LORD bless you and keep you; the LORD make his face to shine upon you and be gracious to you; the LORD lift up his countenance upon you and give you peace" (Numbers 6:23-26).

- "Grace to you and peace from God our Father and the Lord Jesus Christ" (Romans 1:7).

- "May the God of hope fill you with all joy and peace in believing, so that by the power of the Holy Spirit you may abound in hope"(Romans 15:13).

- "May the God of peace be with you all. Amen" (Romans 15:33).

- "The grace of the Lord Jesus Christ and the love of God and the fellowship of the Holy Spirit be with you all" (2 Corinthians 13:14).

- "The grace of our Lord Jesus Christ be with your spirit…Amen" (Galatians 6:18).

- "Now may the Lord of peace himself give you peace at all times and in every way. The Lord be with you all. The grace of our Lord Jesus Christ be with you all" (2 Thessalonians 3:16-18).

- "Now may the God of peace who brought again from the dead our Lord Jesus, the great shepherd of the sheep, by the blood of the eternal covenant, equip you with everything good that you may do his will, working in us that which is pleasing in his sight, through Jesus Christ, to whom be glory forever and ever. Amen" (Hebrews 13:20-21).

- "The God of all grace, who has called you to his eternal glory in Christ, will himself restore, confirm, strengthen, and establish you. To him be the dominion forever and ever. Amen" (I Peter 5:10-11).

- "May grace and peace be multiplied to you in the knowledge of God and of Jesus our Lord. His divine power has granted to us all things that pertain to life and godliness, through the knowledge of him who called us to his own glory and excellence, by which he has granted to us his precious and very great promises, so that through them you may become partakers of the divine nature, having escaped from the corruption that is in the world because of sinful desire" (2 Peter 1:2-4).

- "Grace, mercy, and peace will be with us, from God the Father and from Jesus Christ the Father's Son, in truth and love" (2 John 3).

You can learn more about the practice of blessing on our website, in the *How to Bless Your Children* booklet.

Notes

9

Soldiers of the Cross

In a Nutshell...

Raising children in the faith is a serious, high-stakes endeavor not unlike preparing for battle.

Strong Reactions

Be honest now - how did you react to the title of this chapter?

Over the years, I have noticed a shift in how people react to the idea of being a soldier of the cross. Especially in younger generations, more and more people tend to think differently about war than older generations do. They are very leery about using war metaphors when it comes to their Christian faith, and the idea of being a "soldier of the cross" makes them think of Crusaders, violence, and bloodshed.

Today, we are going to tackle passages in the New Testament that use a lot of war imagery and compare believers to soldiers in an epic battle against evil. It's important to be honest about our reactions so that we can wrestle together with what the Bible says and ultimately become better parents.

Know this: If you reacted negatively, you're not alone. At a family retreat a few years ago, I played a video clip to the parents showing combat scenes from Afghanistan. What I wanted to communicate is this: *How would you be feeling if tomorrow you were sending a son or daughter into combat? Wouldn't you want your child to be thoroughly prepared before leaving for war?* Well, one of the fathers came up afterward and expressed concern, dismayed that I seemed to be glorifying violence. We had a really great discussion about it. In the end, we found common ground: he realized that I was trying to communicate how urgent spiritual parenting is. Sometimes, we need strong metaphors to be able to understand just what's at stake when it comes to raising children.

When we talk about raising soldiers of the cross, we are not advocating for destroying our enemies with violence. We are talking about raising children who understand the nature of the spiritual battle with sin, are well-prepared to engage and are willing to stand for truth. Hopefully, that's something we all want for our children.

Read this Now 1 Peter 5:8-11; Ephesians 6:10-13

Understanding the Battle

Early Christians in the first century after Christ understood the nature of the battle in which they were involved.

I love how the apostle Peter describes it: "Be sober-minded; be watchful. Your adversary the devil prowls around like a roaring lion, seeking someone to devour" (1 Pet. 5:8). If we really believed that about the enemy, I bet we would take our walk with God a little more seriously!

In the face of such a formidable opponent, we definitely need to make sure we are prepared for the fight. That's why Paul encourages us in Ephesians to "take up the whole armor of God, that you may be able to withstand in the evil day, and having done all, to stand firm" (Eph. 6:13).

So now you know the battle exists… but do you know how to identify the constant barrage of attacks against you? Unfortunately, many Christians don't. The good news is that you can train yourself to see them. It starts by opening your eyes, staying close to Jesus, and looking for those things that pull you away from Him. This could be peer pressure to do something wrong. It could be a heart issue like pride, envy, greed, or lust. It could be the voice in our heads that tells us we're not good enough for God's love. It could be any activity that distracts us from our relationship with God or becomes more important than Him. It could be our money or possessions. All of these are tactics of the enemy that hurt our relationship with our Savior.

Paul & Timothy

So if the battle the enemy wages against us is fierce and we have to be ready at all times, what does that mean for parents?

The apostle Paul leads by example in his relationship with Timothy, a young pastor-in-training.

"Wage the good warfare," he instructs. "Fight the good fight... Share in suffering as a good soldier of Christ Jesus" (1 Tim. 1:18, 6:12, 2:3).

And why does Paul have the authority to say this to Timothy? Because he has already experienced the battle! "For I am already being poured out as a drink offering, and the time of my departure has come. I have fought the good fight, I have finished the race, I have kept the faith. Henceforth there is laid up for me the crown of righteousness, which the Lord, the righteous judge, will award to me on that day, and not only to me but also to all who have loved his appearing" (2 Tim. 4:6-8).

As Paul mentors and disciples the young Timothy, he takes on the role of an experienced commanding officer, commissioning and equipping him to take his place on the battlefield. As he approaches the end of his life, Paul desires the same kind of lifelong devotion to the Lord from the young man he has trained.

As Christian parents, our goal for our children should be no less than Paul's desire for Timothy. In fact, while Paul took a large role in Timothy's faith development, he also recognized the role of the parents in this task of evangelizing and discipling. "I am reminded of your sincere faith," Paul told Timothy, "a faith that dwelt first in your grandmother Lois and your mother Eunice and now, I am sure, dwells in you as well" (2 Timothy 1:5).

Notice that Timothy's dad is not mentioned. This may well be why Paul stepped into the gap to help train him, and we can learn something from this today. When fathers are present, they need to take responsibility for training their children. When dads are absent, a mentor should be willing to step in and help. Churches that are wise will recruit Godly men to help fill this role.

Preparing for Battle

Preparing our children for battle isn't easy - but we can do this in two primary ways:

1) Follow the Lord with rock steady devotion.

If you are not a committed soldier of the cross, it will be very hard for you to motivate your child to be one. Remember that kids have a built-in hypocrisy meter - they'll be able to tell if your faith isn't genuine.

2) Take seriously the task of training our children.

Our kids need to know how serious the battle is. Teach them to identify the attacks and distractions of sin, and to take every thought captive, evaluating if it glorifies God or not. They also need to be armed and trained to withstand these attacks. For that, the best tool we have is God's Word. The more our children know the Scriptures, the better equipped they are to stand up for truth. Maybe our homes should look a little like "boot camp", with moms and dads drilling children in the Scripture.

Remaking our families as boot camps will take courage because training our children means we have to talk about hard subjects and be honest about where we fail along the way. But courageous parents raise courageous kids, ready and equipped to battle sin.

Ready, Set, Discuss

How have you seen the attacks of sin and the enemy on your children?

_____

_____

_____

How does the language of battlefields impact how you understand your role in your children's spiritual life?

_____

_____

_____

Now You Try!

Introduce your children to heroes of the faith who weren't perfect, but stood for truth. You can choose characters from the Bible (Daniel, Esther, Stephen, or Paul) or from church history (Dietrich Bonhoeffer, Gladys Aylward, or Mother Teresa).

Notes

_____

_____

_____

_____

_____

10

Generation to Generation

I must admit, I'm a bit of a science geek. I'm sure we all know at least the basics about how genetic traits can be passed from one generation to another via DNA. However, did you know that among animals another form of intergenerational communication exists? In certain situations, learned behavior (not just genetic traits) can be passed to offspring and sometimes, even to different species.

The blue tit, a small songbird with bright blue plumage and a yellow breast native to Europe, offers a humorous example of this intergenerational passing of learned behavior from parent to offspring. Somehow a blue tit in a small area in the north of Great Britain discovered that it was possible to peck open the top of milk bottles left on doorsteps. In just a few years, the thievery spread throughout the country. The spread occurred because somehow, the birds taught both their own young and other species of birds all across Europe how to get free milk.

In humans, something of the same sort seems to happen in the communication of acquired practices, behaviors and beliefs between generations. Stuart Lieberman wrote about this in his book *Transgenerational Family Therapy*[4]. He noted that transmissions from

---

[4] Lieberman, S. (1980). *Transgenerational family therapy*. Kent, UK: Croom Helm.

one generation of humans to the next can be planned, incidental, or even accidental.

Transgenerational Grace

When I read this book, I immediately thought about God's promise in Psalm 112. "Blessed is the man who fears the LORD, who greatly delights in his commandments! His offspring will be mighty in the land; the generation of the upright will be blessed" (Psalm 112:1-2).

This passage helps us understand why the phenomenon of transmitted faith works within vibrant Christian families. It is the principle of *transgenerational grace*. Simply put, God delights to show grace down through the generations of those who do not forget him. Children born into vibrant Christian homes are far more likely to embrace Christ and walk with Him throughout their lives.

If you need more proof, just look to the narrative of Scripture. Starting in the book of Genesis, the truth of transgenerational grace is made very clear. From Adam to Seth, from Seth to Noah, from Noah to Abraham, the first 12 chapters detail God passing the covenant of grace from generation to generation. But it doesn't stop there. From Abraham to Isaac, from Isaac to Jacob, from Jacob to his sons and their children, the book of Genesis ends with a great number who are part of God's covenant of grace. And we see this trend continue throughout the Old Testament, never faltering, all the way until Jesus. All of this because God is a generational God who loves to pass grace through parents to children. He keeps what He has promised in the covenant.

Are parents an important factor? Of course. But underneath all a parent's efforts must be this one sure conviction: God is a remarkable God of grace who delights to give that grace from generation to generation. This is God's promise again and again in the covenant of grace. And our God is faithful to His promises.

Read this Now Psalm 78:2-8, 79:13

Cycle-Breakers

Really, both the above passages should be considered a pair. These psalms of Asaph both talk about the Babylonian captivity. God's people had strayed far from the Lord and God brought judgment as many were captured and carried into exile in Babylon far from their homes in Judah. While in exile, God began to do a work of grace among his people. Meeting and worshipping regularly in synagogues started in Babylon and family life was strengthened as the people struggled to maintain their Jewish identity. After 70 years in captivity, God even moved in the hearts of Babylonian kings to finance the return of many of the exiles to their homeland.

These psalms reveal an important principle for our families: *It is never too late to change; no matter your circumstances you can be a cycle breaker.* Pay attention to verse 8 in particular: "They should not be like their fathers, a stubborn and rebellious generation, a generation whose heart was not steadfast, whose spirit was not faithful to God" (Psalm 78:8). Then, Psalm 79 ends with a remarkable statement: "…we your people, the sheep of your pasture, will give thanks to you forever; from generation to generation we will recount your praise" (Psalm 79:13). These verses show how God's grace enables negative family cycles to be broken so that future generations can come to a more beautiful relationship with God and others.

On a Personal Note

You may have come to this study from a family background that was dysfunctional. If so, I identify with you. I know what you are up against. My wife and I both came into marriage from abusive nuclear families. My dad was physically abusive and my wife's father verbally abused her.

When we got married, we had very few positive examples of family life. All we really knew was what we didn't want our family life to be like! That is not very good preparation for marriage, and we struggled a lot. But we came into marriage committed to each other and prayed constantly that the Lord would break the cycles of the past in our family – so that our children would grow up in something better. God was gracious and has been faithful to do that. If you came from a similar situation, He can do this for you as well.

Or maybe, you feel like it's too late to start making some of these kinds of changes in your family. Perhaps you feel you missed your opportunity. Truth is, change must start somewhere and it can begin where you're at – even if you're raising teenagers, your kids are out of the house, or you're already a grandparent. Throughout my years as a pastor, I have seen countless families reverse course dramatically by God's grace. It's never too late.

God's grace through the generations is evident to me, as I have seen my own children do far better at family life than I did. (I am so proud of my children and their spouses!) And, I fully expect my grandkids to do even better yet. Sure, there will be bumps along the way. There will be sin and sorrow and suffering. But in homes where God is not forgotten, the display of His grace never ends!

Final Thoughts

As we see God at work through the generations in the Bible, we are reminded of this glorious truth for God's people of every age: Our God is no less a generational God now than He was then. It would be inconceivable that His gifting of grace would be any less generous now that our Savior has ushered in the new covenant.

Christian parents can bank on these remarkable promises of our great God: God delights to show His steadfast love to thousands. God delights to withhold judgment. God delights to give transgenerational grace to the children of those who believe.

So we end this study on a hopeful note. Parents, when you are discouraged, when you have failed, when you feel that you are not enough, cling to this: the promises of God in the covenant of grace are for us and for our children and for their children after them. If you are intimidated by the responsibility God has given you, just remember it is not up to you. The God who called you to this task is the God who loves showing grace to thousands!

Ready, Set, Discuss

What negative cycles and patterns did you experience in your upbringing? How do you see God graciously breaking the cycle in your family?

How does the Gospel influence your parenting now? How does this compare to your answer at the start of this study?

Now You Try!

Families: Build an "Ebenezer" memorial together.

Start by reading 1 Samuel 7, stopping to linger on verse 12. Ask your family: Why did Samuel stop to build an altar? What was the purpose of the Ebenezer?

Share with them that in the Old Testament, stones were used as reminders. God's people often built altars with them, so that everyone who saw it would be reminded that God was faithful.

Then, go out to your backyard, neighborhood, a nearby creek or a park and collect some rocks of various sizes.

Back at home, take turns reminding each other of ways God has been faithful to your family (how the Lord has helped us). For each story, write a reminder word or phrase on one of the stones stone in sharpie and add it to the stack of rocks.

By the end, you will have your own family Ebenezer: an altar that serves as a visual reminder that "thus far, the Lord has helped us".

Spend some time in prayer, thanking God for His faithfulness and His promises. Dedicate your family to Him.

Notes

_____

_____

_____

_____

_____

_____

_____

_____

_____

_____

_____

_____

_____

_____

Made in the USA
Columbia, SC
17 October 2022

69512273R00040